HOW TO IMPROVE YOUR LOVE LIFE

How to Improve Your Love Life
Walter the Educator

SKB
Silent King Books
A WhichHead Entertainment Imprint

Copyright © 2024 by Walter the Educator

All rights reserved. No part of this book may be reproduced in any manner whatsoever without written permission except in the case of brief quotations embodied in critical articles and reviews.

First Printing, 2024

Disclaimer

The author and publisher offer this information without warranties expressed or implied. No matter the grounds, neither the author nor the publisher will be accountable for any losses, injuries, or other damages caused by the reader's use of this book. Your use of this book acknowledges an understanding and acceptance of this disclaimer.

How to Improve Your Love Life is a little problem solver book by Walter the Educator that belongs to the Little Problem Solver Books Series. Collect them all and more books at WaltertheEducator.com

LITTLE PROBLEM
SOLVER BOOKS

INTRO

Love is one of the most profound emotions that human beings experience. It has been the subject of art, literature, music, and countless other forms of expression throughout history. While love can come naturally, maintaining and improving your love life requires effort, understanding, communication, and continuous personal growth. Whether you are in a long-term relationship, dating, or even single and looking to develop a deeper connection with yourself, improving your love life starts with intentional steps toward emotional and relational well-being. In this little book, we will explore various methods to improve your love life, covering communication, emotional intelligence, self-awareness, relationship-building skills, and more.

How to Improve Your Love Life

The Importance of Communication in Love

One of the cornerstones of any successful romantic relationship is communication. Communication goes beyond just talking to your partner; it involves active listening, empathy, and the ability to express feelings in a way that is respectful and considerate.

How to Improve Your Love Life

1. Active Listening Active listening is the ability to fully focus on your partner when they are speaking. This means giving them your full attention, making eye contact, and responding thoughtfully. Too often, we listen to respond rather than listen to understand. When you actively listen, you are not only understanding your partner's words but also the emotions behind them. This can prevent misunderstandings and build trust.

How to Improve Your Love Life

2. Clear Expression of Feelings Many people struggle with expressing their emotions in a relationship. This can lead to frustration, resentment, and disconnection. Being open about how you feel is essential to a healthy love life. This doesn't mean that you should share every thought without filter, but rather, find a way to express your needs, desires, and concerns in a way that is constructive. Use "I" statements, such as "I feel hurt when..." or "I would love it if we could...," instead of accusatory language like "You never..." or "You always..." This shifts the focus from blaming your partner to sharing your feelings.

How to Improve Your Love Life

3. Non-Verbal Communication Words are important, but non-verbal communication is just as crucial in improving your love life. Your body language, facial expressions, tone of voice, and gestures can all convey emotions more powerfully than words. If you're feeling loving, your partner should be able to sense that not just through what you say, but how you say it. Positive non-verbal communication, such as affectionate touch or a warm smile, reinforces your verbal messages and strengthens your emotional connection.

How to Improve Your Love Life

Emotional Intelligence in Relationships

Emotional intelligence (EI) is the ability to recognize and manage your own emotions and those of others. In romantic relationships, having high emotional intelligence can lead to deeper connections, improved conflict resolution, and greater empathy between partners.

How to Improve Your Love Life

1. Self-Awareness Self-awareness is at the core of emotional intelligence. It means being conscious of your emotional states, thoughts, and behaviors. When you are self-aware, you can identify how you are feeling in the moment and how those feelings may affect your partner or the relationship. For example, if you are feeling stressed about work, you might unintentionally take that frustration out on your partner. Recognizing this and taking steps to manage your stress can prevent unnecessary tension in your love life.

How to Improve Your Love Life

2. Empathy Empathy is the ability to understand and share the feelings of another person. It's about putting yourself in your partner's shoes and seeing things from their perspective. Practicing empathy can improve your relationship because it allows you to respond to your partner's needs with compassion rather than defensiveness. When your partner feels understood, they are more likely to feel valued and appreciated, which strengthens the bond between you.

How to Improve Your Love Life

3. Managing Conflict Disagreements are a natural part of any relationship, but how you handle them can either strengthen or weaken your love life. Emotional intelligence enables you to manage conflict in a healthy way.

How to Improve Your Love Life

This means staying calm, avoiding hurtful words, and focusing on resolving the issue rather than "winning" the argument. It's also important to know when to step back and give each other space to cool down before continuing the discussion. High emotional intelligence leads to more constructive conflict resolution, resulting in a stronger and more harmonious relationship.

How to Improve Your Love Life

Building Trust and Intimacy

Trust and intimacy are fundamental components of a successful love life. Without trust, it is impossible to build a lasting connection. Intimacy, on the other hand, refers to the closeness and emotional bond that couples share. Both require consistent effort and attention.

How to Improve Your Love Life

1. Cultivating Trust Trust is earned over time through honesty, reliability, and transparency. To build trust in a relationship, it is essential to be consistent in your actions and words.

How to Improve Your Love Life

If you make promises, follow through on them. Avoid hiding things from your partner, whether they are small or significant. Trust also means allowing your partner the space to be themselves without fear of judgment or betrayal.

How to Improve Your Love Life

2. Vulnerability Being vulnerable with your partner means allowing them to see your true self, including your fears, insecurities, and weaknesses. Vulnerability is often viewed as a sign of strength in relationships because it fosters intimacy and connection.

How to Improve Your Love Life

When you share your deeper thoughts and emotions with your partner, you invite them into your inner world. This openness builds trust and closeness, which are vital to improving your love life.

How to Improve Your Love Life

3. Physical Intimacy Physical intimacy is not just about sexual connection; it includes all forms of affectionate touch, such as hugging, holding hands, or simply sitting close to each other. Physical touch releases oxytocin, often referred to as the "love hormone," which helps to strengthen emotional bonds.

How to Improve Your Love Life

Maintaining physical intimacy, whether it's through sex or other forms of touch, is key to keeping the spark alive in a relationship. Make an effort to prioritize physical closeness as a way of showing affection and care for your partner.

How to Improve Your Love Life

Personal Growth and Self-Improvement

While a strong relationship requires two people to work together, individual personal growth is equally important. You cannot rely solely on your partner to make you happy or fulfilled. Improving yourself on an individual level can directly enhance your love life.

How to Improve Your Love Life

1. Self-Love Self-love is the foundation of a healthy relationship. If you do not love and respect yourself, it will be difficult to fully love and respect your partner. Self-love involves taking care of your physical, emotional, and mental well-being.

How to Improve Your Love Life

This could mean practicing self-care activities, setting boundaries, pursuing your passions, or seeking therapy to work through personal issues. When you are secure in yourself, you bring a more positive and confident energy to your relationship.

How to Improve Your Love Life

2. Independence and Space While intimacy and connection are important, so is maintaining a sense of independence. In healthy relationships, both partners should have their own interests, hobbies, and friendships outside of the relationship.

How to Improve Your Love Life

This creates a balance where neither partner feels smothered or overly dependent on the other. Giving each other space to grow individually can enhance the relationship by keeping things fresh and preventing feelings of stagnation.

How to Improve Your Love Life

3. Continuous Learning Relationships are dynamic and ever-evolving, which means there is always room for growth and learning. Take the time to learn about relationships, whether it's through reading books, attending workshops, or seeking couples therapy.

How to Improve Your Love Life

Understanding the complexities of love and partnership can give you valuable insights into improving your relationship. Additionally, learning about your partner, what makes them happy, what triggers them, what their dreams are, can deepen your bond and improve your overall love life.

How to Improve Your Love Life

Healthy Boundaries and Respect

Boundaries are essential in maintaining a healthy and fulfilling relationship. They create a framework for what is acceptable behavior and what is not. Respecting each other's boundaries shows that you value and honor your partner's individuality.

How to Improve Your Love Life

1. Setting Boundaries Setting boundaries means clearly communicating your needs and limits to your partner. This could be emotional, physical, or psychological boundaries.

How to Improve Your Love Life

For example, if you need time alone to recharge, let your partner know. Or if there are certain topics that are particularly sensitive for you, express that to avoid unnecessary hurt. Boundaries are not about shutting your partner out but about creating a safe and respectful environment for both individuals in the relationship.

How to Improve Your Love Life

2. Respecting Boundaries Equally important to setting boundaries is respecting them. When your partner communicates their needs or limits, it's important to honor them without taking it personally.

How to Improve Your Love Life

Respecting boundaries builds trust and shows that you care about your partner's well-being. It also prevents feelings of resentment or suffocation that can arise when boundaries are consistently crossed.

How to Improve Your Love Life

3. Mutual Respect Respect is the bedrock of any successful relationship. This means treating your partner with kindness, understanding, and consideration.

How to Improve Your Love Life

It also means valuing their opinions, even if you don't always agree with them. In disagreements, it's important to argue fairly and avoid personal attacks or disrespectful behavior. Mutual respect ensures that both partners feel valued and secure in the relationship.

How to Improve Your Love Life

Keeping the Spark Alive

Long-term relationships often face the challenge of maintaining excitement and passion. Over time, the initial thrill of romance can fade, but there are ways to keep the spark alive.

How to Improve Your Love Life

1. Prioritizing Quality Time One of the best ways to keep the spark alive is to spend quality time together. In today's fast-paced world, it's easy for work, responsibilities, and distractions to take priority over your relationship.

How to Improve Your Love Life

Make a conscious effort to set aside time for just the two of you, whether it's through date nights, weekend getaways, or simply enjoying each other's company at home. Quality time allows you to reconnect and reminds you why you fell in love in the first place.

How to Improve Your Love Life

2. Trying New Things Together Routine can sometimes lead to boredom in a relationship. To keep things exciting, try new activities together.

How to Improve Your Love Life

This could be anything from traveling to a new destination, taking a dance class, or even trying new foods. Sharing new experiences can reignite the excitement and curiosity that often characterize the early stages of a relationship.

How to Improve Your Love Life

3. Surprise and Spontaneity Surprises and spontaneity add an element of fun and unpredictability to a relationship. It doesn't have to be grand gestures; even small surprises like leaving a sweet note, planning an unexpected outing, or making your partner's favorite meal can make them feel loved and appreciated. The key is to show your partner that you're thinking of them in unexpected ways.

How to Improve Your Love Life

Conclusion

Improving your love life is a multifaceted process that requires dedication, patience, and a willingness to grow both individually and as a couple. By focusing on communication, emotional intelligence, trust, intimacy, personal growth, respect, and keeping the spark alive, you can create a deeper and more fulfilling connection with your partner. Love, like anything worth having, takes effort, but the rewards of a healthy, happy relationship are immeasurable. Whether you are in a long-term partnership or just beginning your journey into love, these principles can help you improve your love life and build lasting connections.

ABOUT THE CREATOR

Walter the Educator is one of the pseudonyms for Walter Anderson. Formally educated in Chemistry, Business, and Education, he is an educator, an author, a diverse entrepreneur, and he is the son of a disabled war veteran. "Walter the Educator" shares his time between educating and creating. He holds interests and owns several creative projects that entertain, enlighten, enhance, and educate, hoping to inspire and motivate you. Follow, find new works, and stay up to date with Walter the Educator™

at WaltertheEducator.com

Milton Keynes UK
Ingram Content Group UK Ltd.
UKHW052039251024
450245UK00013B/835